SUBMARINES

JONATHAN SUTHERLAND AND DIANE CANWELL

Gareth Stevens
Publishing

Please visit our web site at: **www.garethstevens.com**
For a free color catalog describing Gareth Stevens Publishing's list of
high-quality books, call 1-800-542-2595 (USA) or 1-800-387-3178 (Canada).

Library of Congress Cataloging-in-Publication Data

Sutherland, Jonathan.
     Submarines / Jonathan Sutherland and Diane Canwell.
          p. cm. — (Amazing ships)
     ISBN: 978-0-8368-8379-4 (lib. bdg.)
     1. Submarines (Ships) I. Canwell, Diane. II. Title.
     V857.S94   2008
     623.825'7—dc22   2007017051

This North American edition first published in 2008 by
Gareth Stevens Publishing
A Weekly Reader® Company
1 Reader's Digest Road
Pleasantville, NY 10570-7000 USA

Produced by Amber Books Ltd., Bradley's Close,
74–77 White Lion Street, London N1 9PF, U.K.

Project Editor: James Bennett
Copy Editors: Natasha Reed, Chris McNab
Design: Colin Hawes

Gareth Stevens managing editor: Mark Sachner
Gareth Stevens editor: Alan Wachtel
Gareth Stevens art direction: Tammy West
Gareth Stevens production: Jessica Yanke

All illustrations courtesy of Art-Tech/Aerospace

Photo Credits:
Art-Tech/Aerospace: 13, 23; Cody Images: 5, 7, 9, 11, 15, 17, 19; Getty Images: 29; US DOD: 21, 25, 27

Printed in the United States of America

1 2 3 4 5 6 7 8 9 11 10 09 08 07

USS HOLLAND

The USS *Holland* was the U.S. Navy's first submarine. She was named after her inventor, John Philip Holland, and was launched in New Jersey in 1897. The *Holland* was the sixth **prototype** submarine, so she was also known as the *Holland VI*. The U.S. Navy put her into service in October 1900.

Gasoline engines

Ballast tanks like this one could be filled with water. They were used to control the submarine's buoyancy.

The **conning tower** was a raised platform used by the crew for observation.

In this picture, the USS *Holland* (front left) and the Russian battleship *Retvizan* enter the New York Navy Yard dry docks in 1901.

The *Holland* shot aerial torpedos, which could be fired into the air.

Torpedo tube. The *Holland* fired Whitehead torpedoes, which were self-propelled torpedoes powered by compressed air.

U9

The *U9* was the leading vessel of a new class of German submarines called U-boats. ("Class" means vessels of the same type.) She was launched and put into service in 1910. After seven combat patrols during World War I, she was surrendered to the Allies in 1918 and broken up for scrap metal in 1919.

Did You Know?
In July 1914, the *U9* reloaded her torpedoes underwater, a first for a submarine.

Periscopes

The *U9*'s propeller was driven by an engine that produced up to 1,000 **horsepower**.

The air intake tube provided fresh air for the crew when the U-boat was sailing close to the surface.

Gasoline tanks

Stern torpedo tubes

As the *U9* sets sail on a patrol, members of her crew prepare for the voyage on deck. She had a very small crew — only 28 men. By the end of the war, she was outdated.

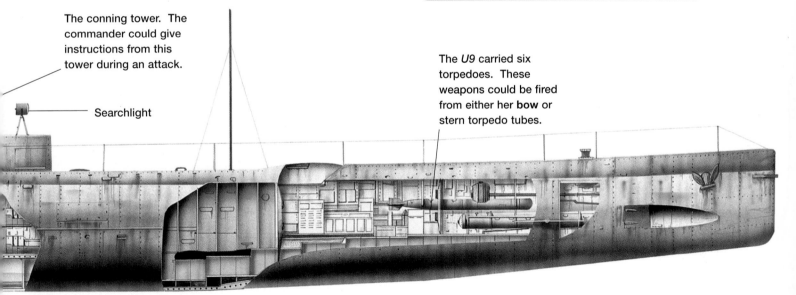

The conning tower. The commander could give instructions from this tower during an attack.

Searchlight

The *U9* carried six torpedoes. These weapons could be fired from either her **bow** or stern torpedo tubes.

HMS E11

The HMS *E11* was the most successful British Royal Navy submarine of World War I. She was launched in April 1914. She was used in the Baltic Sea, but her most famous hunting ground was the Mediterranean Sea. About 58 E-class submarines were built, but none were as famous as the *E11* and her crew.

The *E11* had two propellers, one on each side. These gave her a maximum speed of 14 **knots** (26 kilometers per hour) on the surface and 5 knots (9 kph) underwater.

A **bulkhead**. The E-class subs were fitted with internal watertight bulkheads. These were used to stop water from spreading through the submarine in a flood.

Main engine. The *E11* mixed diesel and electric power.

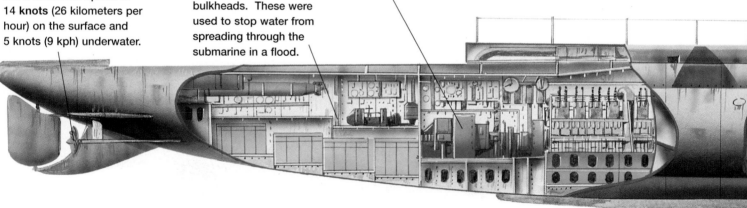

The conning tower featured the *E11*'s periscopes and an air-intake tube.

An enemy shell hit the top section of this **periscope** in 1915.

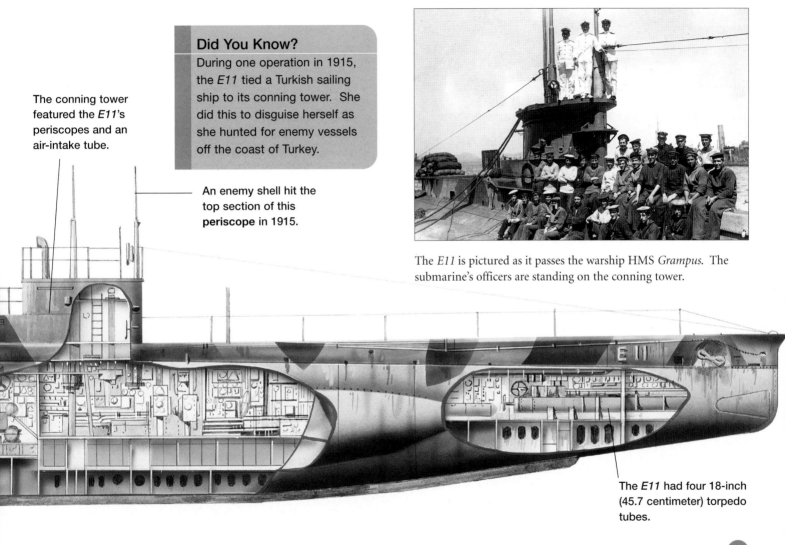

The *E11* is pictured as it passes the warship HMS *Grampus*. The submarine's officers are standing on the conning tower.

The *E11* had four 18-inch (45.7 centimeter) torpedo tubes.

DEUTSCHLAND

The German cargo-carrying submarine *Deutschland* was built in 1916 to break the British blockade on German ports during World War I. The *Deutschland* made its first voyage to Baltimore, Maryland, in July 1916, covering the distance in two weeks. (At the time, Germany and the United States were still trading.) On the outbound voyage, she carried dyes, precious stones, and mail. She brought back nickel, silver, and zinc. She made the entire trip unarmed.

Did You Know?
The *Deutschland*'s sister ship, the *Bremen*, left for Norfolk, Virginia, in August 1916, but was lost without a trace.

Crane for lifting goods from the hold onto the docks

The *Deutschland* could carry 700 tons (635 metric tons) of goods in her hold.

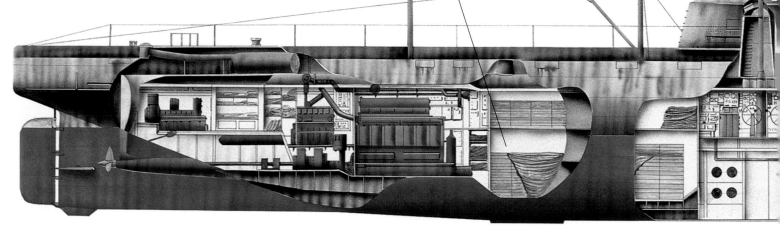

The *Deutschland* returns to Bremen, Germany, after its journey to the United States in July 1916.

A crew cabin. In total, the living quarters held four officers and 25 other naval crew.

When she was turned into a war submarine, the *Deutschland* was fitted with two 19.7-inch (50 cm) torpedo tubes in her bow.

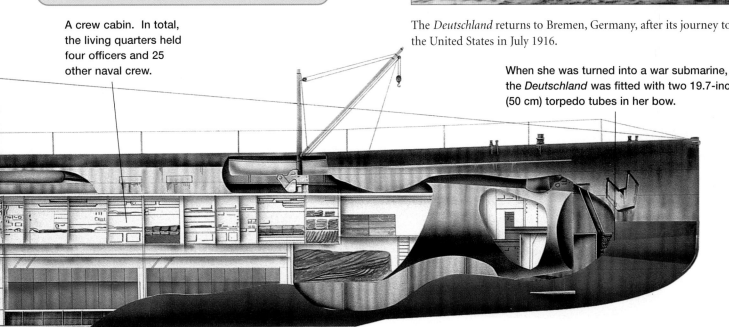

SURCOUF

Work began on this French submarine in 1929, and she was completed in 1934. The *Surcouf* was designed as an underwater cruiser, and she weighed 280 tons. She was sunk in February 1942 when she collided with a U.S. ship in the Gulf of Mexico. Neither vessel had lights on, so they did not spot one another until it was too late. The U.S. ship survived.

KEY FACTS

• The *Surcouf* was the heaviest submarine in service during World War I.

• She had the largest guns allowed by the Washington Naval Treaty, an agreement signed by Great Britain, the United States, France, Japan, and Italy in 1922 to limit the size of naval weapons.

The *Surcouf* had a pair of 8-inch (20.3 cm) guns mounted in a turret on the deck.

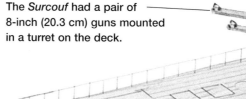

Torpedo tubes. The *Surcouf* carried 22 torpedoes.

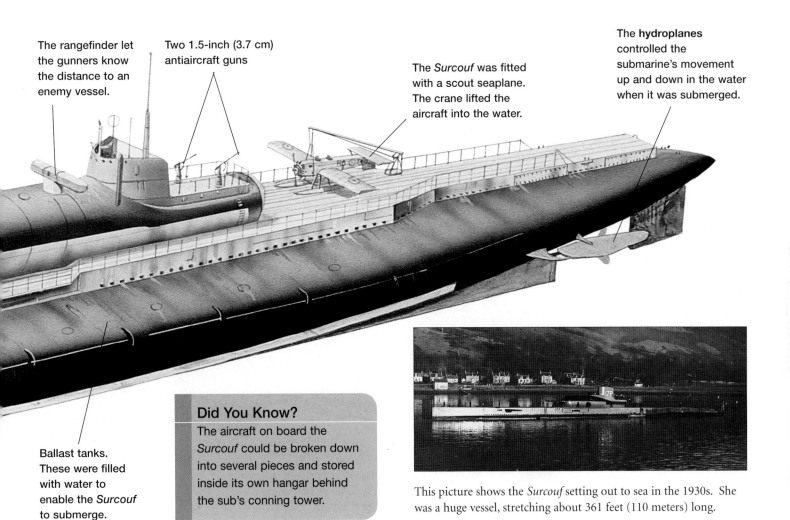

The rangefinder let the gunners know the distance to an enemy vessel.

Two 1.5-inch (3.7 cm) antiaircraft guns

The *Surcouf* was fitted with a scout seaplane. The crane lifted the aircraft into the water.

The **hydroplanes** controlled the submarine's movement up and down in the water when it was submerged.

Ballast tanks. These were filled with water to enable the *Surcouf* to submerge.

Did You Know?
The aircraft on board the *Surcouf* could be broken down into several pieces and stored inside its own hangar behind the sub's conning tower.

This picture shows the *Surcouf* setting out to sea in the 1930s. She was a huge vessel, stretching about 361 feet (110 meters) long.

U-Boat Type VIIC

German Type VIIC submarines were built between 1933 and 1945. They were the most numerous U-boat type ever built, and a total of 568 were put into service. The first was *U69*, which was built in 1940. Type VIIC submarines did huge damage during World War II, but the Allies sank most of them in the last three years of the war.

The radio aerial allowed communication between U-boats. Communication was essential for a group of U-boats attacking a large convoy of ships.

The propellers were powered by 2,800 horsepower diesel engines and a 750 horsepower electric engine.

The Type VIIC had two propeller shafts, one on each side.

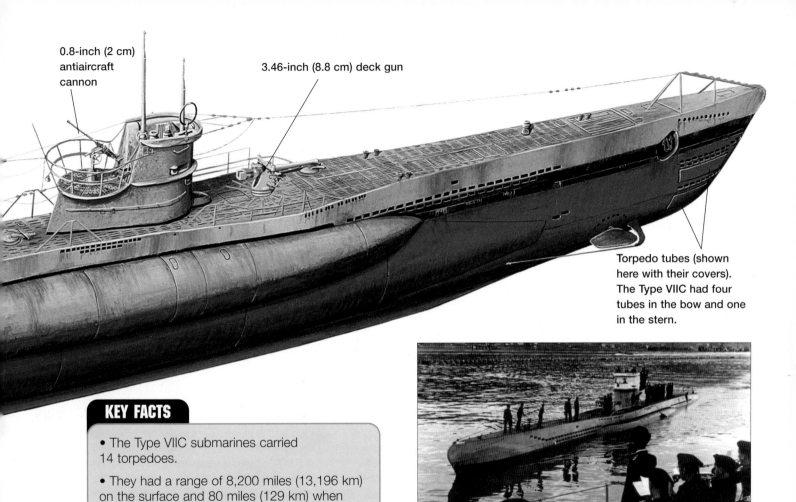

0.8-inch (2 cm) antiaircraft cannon

3.46-inch (8.8 cm) deck gun

Torpedo tubes (shown here with their covers). The Type VIIC had four tubes in the bow and one in the stern.

KEY FACTS

• The Type VIIC submarines carried 14 torpedoes.

• They had a range of 8,200 miles (13,196 km) on the surface and 80 miles (129 km) when submerged.

• Most Type VIIC submarines had a crew of between 44 and 52 men.

A German Type VII U-boat is given a musical send-off from a U-boat station on the Baltic coast of northern Europe.

U-BOAT TYPE XXI

The German World War II Type XXI, or "Elektroboote," submarines were the first submarines designed for operating mainly underwater. (Most submarines up to this time spent more time on the surface than submerged.) To keep the crew comfortable while submerged, the Type XXI had freezers for food and hot-water showers. Between 1943 and 1945, 118 Type XXI U-boats were built.

The submarine's 1.4-inch (3.5 cm) twin antiaircraft guns could be pulled back inside the ship before it went underwater.

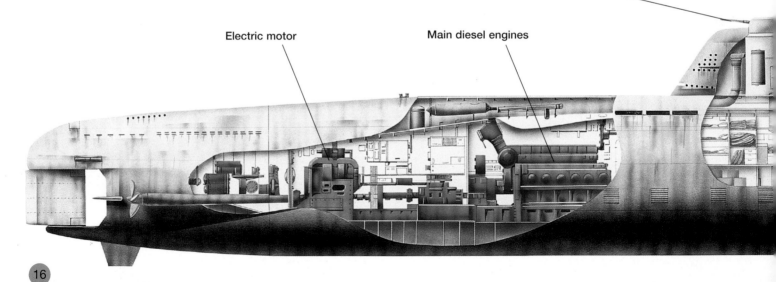

Electric motor

Main diesel engines

The Allies tested eight Type XXIs after the war. These influenced U.S., British, French, and Russian postwar submarine designs.

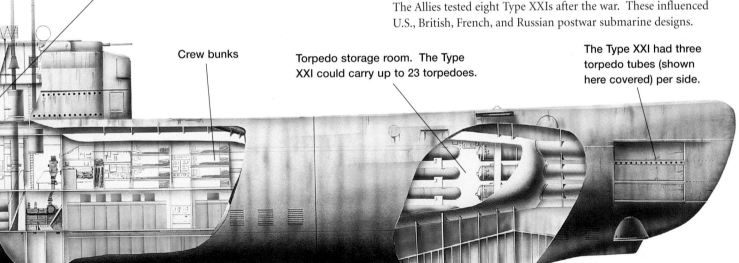

Control room

Crew bunks

Torpedo storage room. The Type XXI could carry up to 23 torpedoes.

The Type XXI had three torpedo tubes (shown here covered) per side.

ZEELEEUW

The Royal Netherlands Navy vessel called the *Zeeleeuw* was originally a U.S. Navy ship. She was called the USS *Hawkbill*, and was launched in Manitowoc, Wisconsin, in January 1944. As the *Hawkbill*, she saw action with the U.S. Navy in the Pacific against Japan between 1944 and 1945. She joined the U.S. Reserve Fleet in 1946 and was loaned to the Netherlands in 1953, when she was given the name *Zeeleeuw*.

KEY FACTS

• By the end of World War II, the USS *Hawkbill* had received six battle star awards, each given for service in a different campaign.

• The *Hawkbill* sank her first ship, the Japanese destroyer *Momo*, in December 1944.

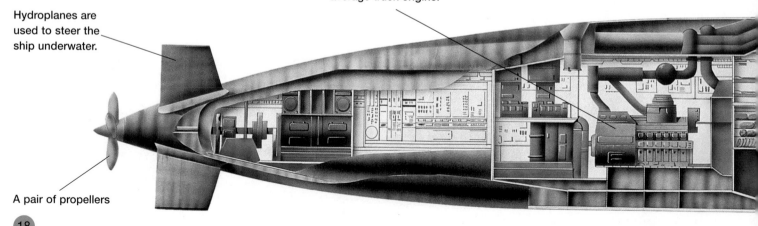

Main engines. The submarine was propelled by four 5,400-horsepower diesel engines and four 2,740-horsepower electric engines. Each diesel engine was more than ten times more powerful than the average truck engine.

Hydroplanes are used to steer the ship underwater.

A pair of propellers

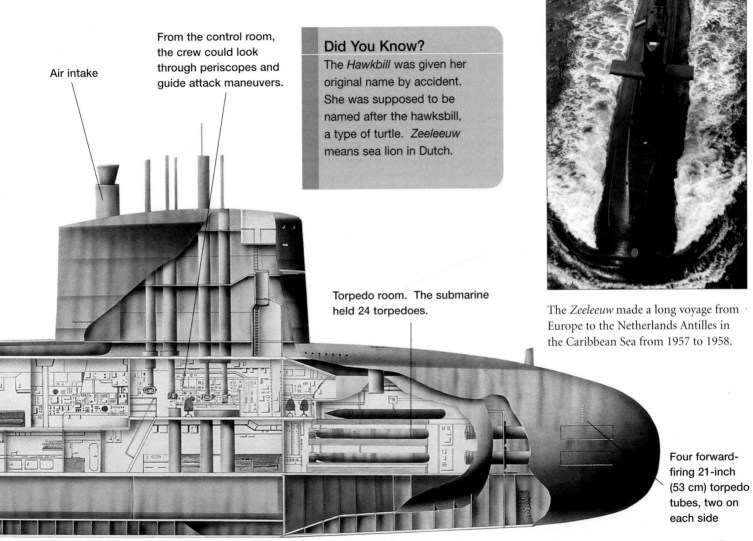

Air intake

From the control room, the crew could look through periscopes and guide attack maneuvers.

Torpedo room. The submarine held 24 torpedoes.

The *Zeeleeuw* made a long voyage from Europe to the Netherlands Antilles in the Caribbean Sea from 1957 to 1958.

Four forward-firing 21-inch (53 cm) torpedo tubes, two on each side

USS NAUTILUS

The USS *Nautilus* was the world's first nuclear-powered submarine. She was launched from Connecticut in January 1954. Her first secret mission was to cross beneath the North Pole, which she did in 1958. In 1960, she became the first nuclear-powered submarine to be sent to operate in the Mediterranean.

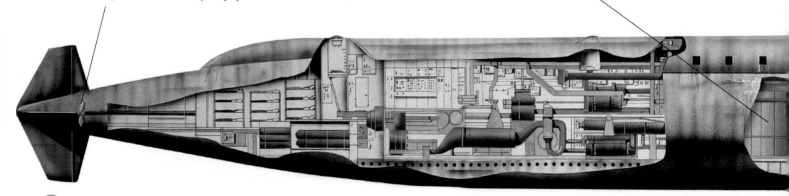

A pair of propellers can push the submarine to an underwater speed of 23 knots (43 kph).

The pressured water-cooled **nuclear reactor** powered a pair of steam turbine engines.

The *Nautilus* is so important in U.S. naval history that the U.S. government named her a National Historic Landmark in 1982.

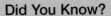

An advanced **sonar** tracker used sound waves for locating ships to be targeted.

The attack center. From here, the crew controlled the ship during torpedo runs.

The control room

One of six 21-inch (53 cm) torpedo tubes

HMS RESOLUTION

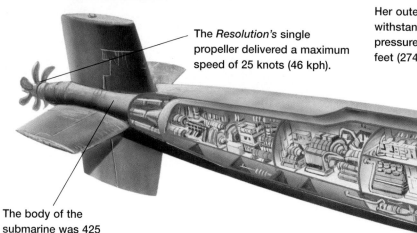

The *Resolution's* single propeller delivered a maximum speed of 25 knots (46 kph).

Her outer body could withstand water pressure down to 900 feet (274 m).

A Polaris nuclear missile in its launcher. The *Resolution* was armed with 16 Polaris missiles that could be launched from special ports on the top of the submarine.

The body of the submarine was 425 feet (129.5 m) long.

HMS *Resolution* was the first Resolution-class submarine built for the British Royal Navy. Designed to carry Polaris nuclear missiles, she was launched in 1966 and came into service in 1967. Her construction was unusual because, although she was a British submarine, the section containing her missiles and their control system was made in the United States, separately from the rest of the vessel.

Did You Know?

In the James Bond film *The Spy Who Loved Me (1977)*, the hijacked submarine was a Resolution-class submarine.

- HMS *Resolution* test-fired her first Polaris missile in February 1968.

- Throughout their service, the four Resolution-class submarines were based in Scotland.

- The *Resolution* spent 28 years on patrol.

A British Resolution-class submarine test launches a Polaris missile. These missiles were taken out of service in 1996.

Six 21-inch (53 cm) torpedo tubes

The crew berths, where the crew slept and kept their personal belongings. The *Resolution* had a full crew of 143.

USS LOS ANGELES

The USS *Los Angeles* was the first of many American Los Angeles-class nuclear-powered attack submarines. She was launched in 1974 and came into service in 1976. Los Angeles-class submarines became the most numerous single type of nuclear submarine built by any nation.

The nuclear reactor was housed in this thick-walled compartment for safety.

Radio room

Did You Know?

The *Los Angeles* was the fourth U.S. Navy ship to be named after the city. The others were a tanker, a heavy cruiser, and a German-built airship.

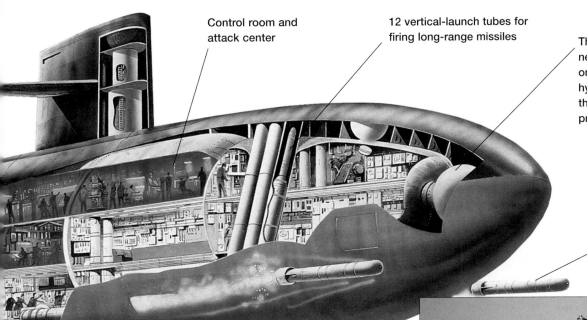

Control room and attack center

12 vertical-launch tubes for firing long-range missiles

The sonar sphere has nearly 1,000 **hydrophones** on its surface. These hydrophones can detect the noise of a ship's propeller from miles away.

The *Los Angeles's* Mk 48 torpedoes can destroy surface ships and submarines from more than 5 miles (8 km) away.

KEY FACTS

• Wherever the submarine was located, its missiles could hit a target on 75 percent of Earth's surface.

• The Los Angeles-class submarines are all named after cities in the United States.

Crew members of the USS *Los Angeles* stand on deck as the ship comes into port. The *Los Angeles* has a crew of about 140.

USS OHIO

The *Ohio* was originally designed to fire Trident missiles (shown here). She was upgraded in 2003–2005 to fire Tomahawk cruise missiles.

A two-geared steam turbine that is powered by the nuclear reactor

The nuclear reactor needs refueling every nine years.

Each of the 22 launch tubes on board the upgraded *Ohio* carries seven Tomahawk cruise missiles.

The USS *Ohio* was the first of the Trident class of nuclear-powered submarines. (This class of sub got its name from the Trident nuclear missiles they were designed to carry.) It was launched in April 1979. In 2003, it was converted to carry 154 Tomahawk cruise missiles instead of 24 Trident missiles. The *Ohio* is the largest submarine ever made for the U.S. Navy. It is second in size only to Russian Typhoon-class vessels, the largest class of submarine ever built.

KEY FACTS

• The *Ohio* is sometimes used to support U.S. Special Forces operations, deploying elite soldiers near enemy coastlines.

• The *Ohio* was due to be retired in 2002, but her conversion to carry Tomahawk cruise missiles has kept her in service.

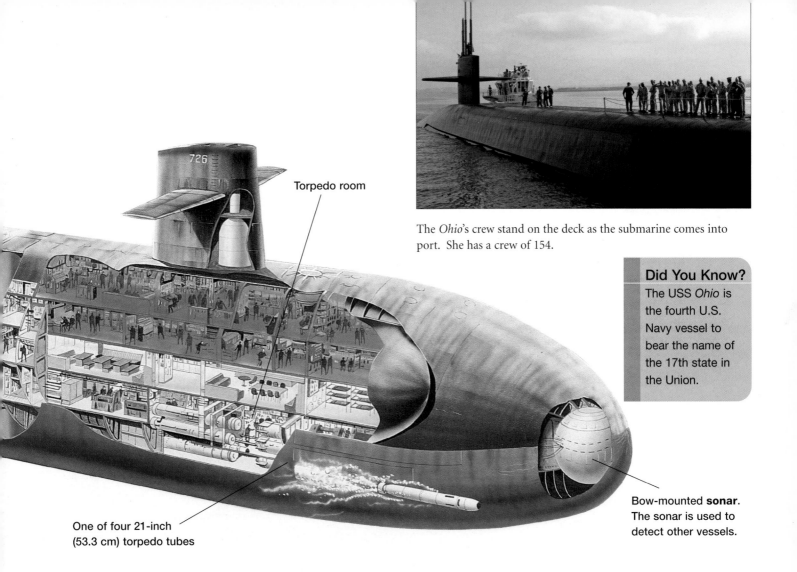

Torpedo room

The *Ohio*'s crew stand on the deck as the submarine comes into port. She has a crew of 154.

One of four 21-inch (53.3 cm) torpedo tubes

Bow-mounted **sonar**. The sonar is used to detect other vessels.

KURSK (K-141)

The *K-141 Kursk* was a Russian nuclear sub that was launched in 1994. She sank in August 2000, and all her whole crew was killed. The disaster occurred at a time of cutbacks for Russia's fleet. Hardly any maintenance had been carried out on her. Many of her parts, including torpedoes, had rusted. In August 2000, explosions occured inside *Kursk*. She sank to the ocean floor in the icy waters of the Barents Sea.

KEY FACTS

• The *Kursk* was 508 feet (154.8 m) long.

• There were two explosions aboard the *Kursk*. The first torpedo explosion caused a major fire, which later set off other torpedo warheads. The second explosion blew open the hull, letting in thousands of tons of seawater.

• Twenty-three out of the crew of 118 survived the explosions, but they were trapped in a compartment and died when their air ran out.

The Kursk had two hulls. There was a 7-foot (2.1 m) gap between the outer hull and the inner hull, and both were made from 2-inch (5 cm) thick steel.

A pair of nuclear reactors and two steam turbines

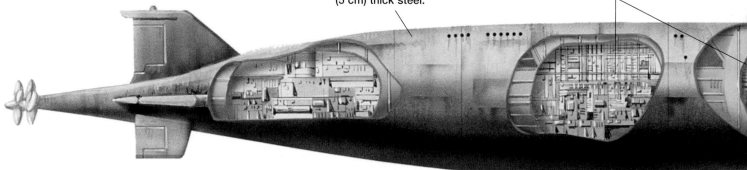

The Dutch salvage ship shown here raised the *Kursk*. This ship's crew managed to recover the bodies of 115 of the *Kursk's* crew.

A missile **launch tube**. The *Kursk* was capable of firing 24 nuclear missiles.

Living quarters. The *Kursk* had a crew of about 120 officers and enlisted sailors.

The *Kursk's* torpedo room was stacked with 21-inch (53.3 cm) and 25.6-inch (67.3 cm) torpedoes.

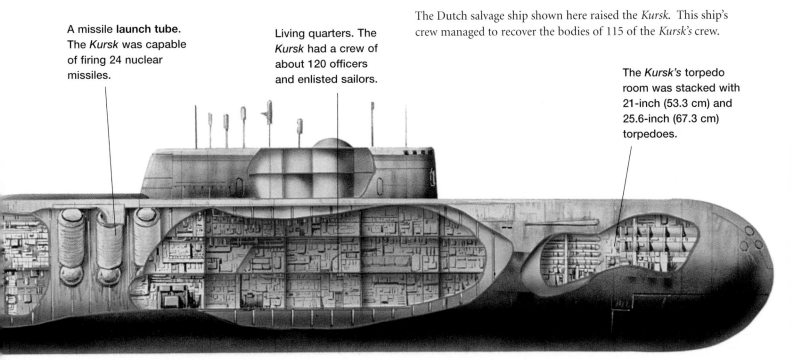

GLOSSARY

ballast tank in a submarine, a tank that can be filled with water to enable the craft to dive underwater or air to enable it to return to the surface

bow the front part of a ship

bulkhead a vertical wall that divides up a ship or submarine into separate compartments

conning tower a raised platform on a ship or submarine on which an officer stands to give steering or other instructions

horsepower a unit of measurement for the power of an engine

hull the main body of a ship that is built to allow it to float

hydrophone an underwater microphone that picks up sound and uses it to locate objects in the water

hydroplanes on a submarine, hinged winglike structures on the hull that are used to steer the ship underwater

knot a unit for measuring the speed of ships that is equivalent to 1.1 miles per hour (1.8 kph)

launch tube a tube through which a missile is fired

nuclear reactor a device that uses nuclear reactions to produce electrical power

periscope a device that uses a series of mirrors and prisms to allow someone to look at something that is not in their line of sight

prototype the first model of something, which are tested and improved to lead to the final production model

sonar a system that uses sound waves to detect objects in the water, such as other submarines or boats

stern the rear part of a ship or submarine

torpedo a long, tubular weapon that once fired travels through the water and explodes against or near a ship or submarine

FOR MORE INFORMATION

BOOKS

- *Life on a Submarine.* On Duty (series). Gregory Payan and Alexander Guelke (Children's Press)

- *Submarine.* Eyewitness Guides (series). Neil Mallard (DK Children)

- *Submarines.* Military Hardware in Action (series). Kevin Doyle (Lerner Publications)

- *Submarines.* Step Into Reading (series). Sydelle Kramer (Random House)

- *Submarines: Underwater Stealth.* Mighty Military Machines (series). Michael Teitelbaum (Enslow Publishers)

WEB SITES

- NavSource Naval History: Photographic History of the U.S. Navy
  www.navsource.org

- Haze Gray and Underway: Naval History and Photography
  www.hazegray.org

- Warship: Submarines
  www.pbs.org/wnet/warship/submarines/index.html

- How Stuff Works: How Submarines Work
  www.science.howstuffworks.com/submarine.htm

- Office of the Chief of Naval Operations: Submarine Warfare Division
  www.navy.mil/navydata/cno/n87/n77.html

Publisher's note to educators and parents:

Our editors have carefully reviewed these Web sites to ensure that they are suitable for children. Many web sites change frequently, however, and we cannot guarantee that a site's future contents will continue to meet our high standards of quality and educational value. Be advised that children should be closely supervised whenever they access the internet.

INDEX